A Lakeland(shire) Lad
by Steve Ziemba

First Printing

This book is dedicated to all of those that encouraged me both emotionally and intellectually to complete this work.
Your support is much appreciated and will never be forgotten.

Forward

If you picked up this book because the title sounded similar to A. E. Housman's poetry book The Shropshire Lad, then this book is for you. I am a poet in the rhyming tradition, and Dorothy Parker and A. E. Housman are not only my two favorite poets, but had a big influence on my writing. I'm not sure when the trend began that started to eliminate rhyming poetry in favor of free verse but today the transition is pretty much complete. On many college campuses today, free verse is what is taught. I have even read of one college professor who is asking his students why they should confine and limit themselves to rhyming words and a metering cadence when they have the whole English language to express themselves in? That's probably a fair question but I would reply that using rhyming words to express yourself in a structured and metered cadence is a skill that not many can do. Expressing yourself in free verse, or what I call "prosetry", is much easier to do for the masses. But that's exactly why I call rhyming poetry a skill. Promoting free verse in place of rhyme to me is like saying why don't we adjust the height of the basketball hoop to five feet so everyone can slam dunk? Sure, everyone can now slam dunk but certainly the skill, and therefore the excitement, is gone. I certainly think there is a place for both types of poetry in this world. My place is on the rhyming side of the spectrum.

I started writing poetry in my late teens and continued until I was into my late twenties. Thankfully, little of it survives today to threaten mankind. When the COVID isolation came upon us, I picked up my pen and started writing again. The biggest difference of course is that I no longer use a pen or pencil. Using a keyboard is so much easier today than how it used to be. The second difference is that in comparing what I write today to some of my earlier works long ago, I find that today's poems are much deeper in thought and meaning than my prior works. A friend told me that was because I have been through far more life experiences that shaped my writing. She is correct of course and some of the works I have done today I would never have even thought about doing way back then.

So, what will you find in these pages? When people ask me what I write about, I tell them I write about life, and life isn't always pretty. Therefore, in these pages you will find the humorous poems, love poems, and the poems that make observations about life in general. But you will also find poems about lost love, deep loneliness, depression, suicide and even the trauma of date rape. You will also find poems that you may think you know what is going on but at the very last stanza, maybe even the very last line, you will realize the poem isn't about what you thought it was. I love doing misdirectional poems every now and then just to keep the readers from thinking that they have me all figured out. Why did I include these much darker works? Because as I said, life isn't always pretty and I feel that these subjects need to be written about and not swept under the rug somewhere. I also want to challenge the reader and to bring out their emotions. In my view that's what good poetry does. Good poetry isn't always about sunshine and butterflies. Many times it is thought provoking, heart wrenching, and leaves the reader sitting there having to come to terms with their emotions about what they just read. I hope I succeeded in that regard.

People often tell me that they like my poems because they tell a story and I certainly can understand that. For the vast majority of my work, I write the ending or near ending first. Once I know where I want to go, I write the beginning and middle to get there. That produces the "story" effect that is so often apparent in my work. People have also asked me many times if I am the subject of my poems. Yes, many are autobiographical. For others, my own experiences have given me the inspiration and thought process for the poem, but I don't necessarily feel the way the subject feels in the poem. I am always surprised at how many poems I have written where the end result is far removed from what I originally envisioned. As for those poems that are not autobiographical or self inspired from my own experiences, I feel I have the ability to interject myself into a situation and "feel" what the subject of the poem is feeling. Finally, I have to tell you that I do not interpret my work. I leave that up to the reader. If you, the reader, likes something I have written, I don't want to spoil that in any way for you. Think of it this way. How many times have you heard a song and liked it very much but then found out what the song was really about or why it was written? You may still like the song, but maybe not as much. I don't want to spoil your interpretation of the work and ruin your enjoyment of it. Therefore my rule is: I wrote it, you interpret it.

Finally, if you do like my work and want to tell me, feel free. Maybe it's due to our vanity but artists, which I now consider myself one, always like to hear from their appreciative fans. I have set up an e-mail address at smpz30@yahoo.com. I have no idea how much e-mail I will get from this book but I will try to answer as many as time allows. Until then: Welcome to my world and enjoy your stay.

Steve Ziemba

Table of Contents

What is Love?

It was late at night while I was sitting alone
  When I was approached by my child asking in the inquisitive tone
Said the child "I have a question. Can you answer it please?"
  I thought "Oh no! You're too young to be asking of the birds
  and the bees!".

The child just stood there looking innocent as a dove
  And then the child continued "Can you tell me of this thing
  they call love?"
I replied, "I'll certainly try." as I coaxed the child near me
  And then climbing up on my knee sitting together were we.

I answered, "Love is a stab to the heart and a twist of the knife,
walking the floor and endless strife
A deep seated gloom and tear filled eyes, if you're sick to your
stomach don't be surprised
You can't be consoled your life is a waste and everything around
you leaves a distaste.
A sadness and emptiness deep inside, you really don't care if
you lived or you died."

"So love is bad." the child said. "Not necessarily," I replied, "it
could be this instead."

"You feel as if you're in heaven and angels are flying, everything's great you're so happy you're crying
It's puppies and kittens and every cute cuddly thing and everywhere you go you begin to sing
It's Christmas and July 4th all rolled into one, with the fireworks and sparklers increasing the fun
It's carnivals, candy and your favorite amusement ride, with someone very special right by your side."

I could see that the child I was beginning to confuse
    So I told the child "Look, you don't have to choose
It's not one or the other but a mixture instead
    And when you are older you will understand." I said.

So while off to bed the child went to slumber
    I sat there and pondered and started to wonder
And I couldn't answer this question as night grew colder
    When will **I** understand love, now that I'm the proverbial "older"?

The Lonely Day

As I get out in the morning to make my day
I see couples together closely side by side
Their respect and love for each other can be clearly spied
As they lovingly go about their way.
And I think I would really like to meet someone, if only
To share the morning sun and see the sights
To share the farmers markets and the other delights
Boy mornings can really be lonely.

As I go about my errands in the afternoon
I see couples walking together with arms around each
other's waist
Taking their time and not in any haste
To be anywhere at anytime soon.
And I think I would really like to meet someone, if only
To share the afternoon sun and to take a walk
To hold each other's hand and to make small talk
Boy afternoons can really be lonely.

As I stroll through the evening and make my rounds
I see couples as they are touching and holding
Into each other's arms they are cuddling and folding
And the air is filled with their teasing and laughter sounds.
And I think I would really like to meet someone, if only
To share the evening sun and to watch the moon rise
To share an evening drink as we gaze into each other's eyes
Boy evenings can really be lonely.

Hands of Time

If I could turn back the hands of time
And redirect my life anew
Would changing time be an awful crime
To correct things that I did and didn't do?

To mend some friendships that fell apart
And were ended in too much haste
To give my apologies from the heart
I rue the years that have gone to waste.

The loves I've lost through actions done
To spare the pain and all the sorrow
Instead of love fading under a setting sun
Things would be brighter on the morrow.

To change the direction my life would take
To know what path to walk
To know the true course and not the fake
And what not to mention when I talk.

But they say you are a product of your past
And for me that's the problem as I see.
Since if I took my past and changed the cast
Then that new "I" just wouldn't be me.

The Goddess

I sit here impaled by love's sweet caress
    It's embers stoked by Cupid's fan
But there is no way that her I can impress
    I have no earthly plan
For she is a dark haired, dark eyed Goddess
    And I am merely a man.

She holds my heart so from her I can't flee
    And how to win her I have no clue
But she is the one I'll always be
    Forevermore beholden to
So Goddess I'm sorry you're still stuck with me
    Because Goddess I'm still stuck on you.

Shattered Dreams

What do you do when your dreams are dead
    And are lying broken upon the ground?
How do you dream new dreams instead
    Replacing those that lie scattered around?

What do you do when your hopes are shattered
    All of them torn apart?
Everything shredded that really mattered
    Where do you begin to start?

What do you do when your faith takes a blow
    And you wonder if God even exists?
How can He subject you to this horror show
    With too many horrors to list?

What do you do when your self worth has been ripped
with a knife
    Was it all just a Grand Illusion?
All of the plans you had made for your life
    Now seem only to be a delusion.

What do you do when your emotions have dried
    And any feeling has been put asunder?
Can you simply survive with no feeling inside,
    Can it be that easy? I wonder.

What do you do when your dreams are dead
    How do you start your life anew?
So what do you do when your dreams are dead?
    I really don't know, do you?

The Love Triangle

Dick loves Jane but Jane loves Dirk
    And Dirk loves fast cars and boozin'.

Dick feels bad and Jane feels sad
    And Dirk kills a man while DWI cruisin'.

Dick moved on and Jane went on
    And Dirk's at a jail cell doin' time in.

I guess there really isn't any moral to this rhyme
    'Cept maybe don't go drinkin' and drivin'.

When Death
Comes Knocking

When Death comes knocking at my door
    I shall not run and hide.
I'll throw it open all the more
    And welcome him inside.

I've lived my life as best I could,
    And I really can't complain.
Had my sun filled days like others would
    And those filled with acid rain.

My life won't win any awards you see
    Nor even an Honorable Mention.
And neither fame nor fortune was dealt to me
    So less stress and little tension.

I'll never earn the Arnold hype
    My physique will never match Stallone.
Won't be walking with a Raquel Welch type
    I just ask that I never walk alone.

So when it comes time for me to leave this site
    May they say I had good will towards men
And on my stone please just write
    "He tried to leave this place a little better. RIP. Amen.".

Girl in the Stands

Girl in blue blouse and jeans in the stands
You are thinking in deep contemplation.
What are you so peacefully thinking about
Are you thinking of life and your role in relation?

Your beauty and your wit, your charm and your grace,
Inside of you do you see this collection?
Or when you look in the mirror do you miss all of that
And do you only view your reflection?

When you slowly walk barefoot at night on the beach
In long dress and a low cut bodice,
Does the moon cede to your beauty and does it step aside
Or does it jealously pretend not to notice?

When the wind softly blows and brushes your cheek
And softly ruffles your hair,
Does it do so in order to caress your skin
Which is so soft, so warm and so fair?

Girl in blue blouse and jeans in the stands
You are standing and getting ready to go.
And the thing I regret is that the answers I seek here
To these questions I'll never know.

For Sue

I was talking with an old friend and generally rehashing
The times that we had and the people that we knew
And I fondly remembered and so asked of you
And was very shocked to learn of your passing.

Pondering this news while my feelings grew tender
I realized the time that had passed blurred your image to me
Though I still hear your voice and miss your personality
It was your smile that I still and will always remember.

We who were fooled by youth into thinking us immortal
We who were shocked by our friends who left us early like you
We who witnessed death by illness and accident too
We who were surprised to find we were truly quite mortal.

Still when I heard of your death my heart was leaden
I prayed for your soul after your life's final last act
But then I realized this is being written so far after the fact
That it's long since the time angels whisked you away to
Heaven.

As I am sitting here while pondering and musing
I think that if I do my good deeds before I have died
Then we'll say hello again and we'll hug as I cross to the
other side
This all happening on a day of God's choosing.

Valentine Ode

I reached out and took your hand
Our dinner lit by candlelight
Your dress and hair done up so grand
Your lips so moist so right
Our souls caught up and intertwined
And I'm sure I'm not mistaken
When I tell you that I love you more
Than five pounds of freshly sizzling bacon.

The Young Lovers

The words lead to kissing which gets heavy and hot
    And the hands they all start a roamin'
The passions and fire are pourin' out a lot
    And the voices they start a moanin'

But you're underage girl, you know what I'm talkin' about
    So from that boy I'd certainly skedaddle
Because if tongues start waggin and your father finds out
    Girl it is you that he's a goin' to paddle.

The Don't – Won't Trilogy

*In Consideration of Giving Your Heart to a Guy Who Says He
Will Give You His Heart if Only You Have Sex With Him*

Don't. He won't.

*In Consideration of Giving Your Heart to a Girl Who Says She Will
Give You Her Heart if Only You Buy Her Everything She Wants*

Don't. She won't.

*In Consideration of Giving Your Friendship to a Person or Group
Who Insist
They Will Be Your Friends if You Tell Them All of Your Secrets*

Don't. They won't.

My Little View of the World

The morning is here in all of its glory
    The sun shines bright and clear
And let me tell you of my little story
    Both of what I see and what I hear.

The breeze through the leaves is playing its tune
    A few white clouds float over my deck
And the sun will tell you that it's still pre-noon
    They call that the doppler effect.

The squirrels are out and scavenging for food
    They run up and down every tree
They may give each other some attitude
    But they really don't bother me.

I see the birds flittering, hovering up and down
    They'll fly all over except near me
And the flying insects that are buzzing around
    Make for an interesting cacophony.

My neighbor's chickens are out I guarantee
    Their free ranging you've got to love
And their constant clucking never vexes me
    However that rooster I'd love to hear less of.

Add in to all this is my breakfast meal
    The coffee and the eggs and the bacon
A perfect Saturday morning becoming real
    Never for granted is it taken.

So I sit here peacefully taking in the sight
    With all its scenic beauty unfurled
All of my cares quickly taking flight
    Thanking God for my little view of the world.

Chastity Undone

A virgin was I until that night
Unsuspecting of events to transpire
Innocence shattered, virtue lost in flight
Only deep shame left as my shroud of attire.

He plied me with wine said it was no sin
Whispered sweet talk in my ear
Said if I loved him I'd let him in
Only me he wanted to be near.

His hands were groping I tried to flee
But he forced me down to the floor
Vile disgust welled up inside me
My chastity was to be no more.

Feeling utter rage and raw shame
I cried, pleaded, sick with the rank degradation
Thoughts filled my mind, like was I to blame?
Nauseous with the pain of penetration.

Life used to be so simple and fun
So many things I held so dear
Now the darkness blots out the sun
And pregnancy and STD's I fear.

A nice evening was all I desired...wanted
Not sobbing behind a locked door
I lay in bed feeling dirty, unwanted
A virgin was I...now a virgin no more.

The Breakup

I will have to break a heart today
Tell her there is no chemistry or sparks
I'll have to be cautious with what I say
And with any and all my remarks
No birds will be singing as we walk away
Neither robins nor thrushes nor larks.

So why does it hurt so much to part
With sad emotions that will overflow?
It feels so much like a poison dart
And not Cupid's arrow and bow
I know she'll have sadness in her heart
Only my heart will ache even moreso.

Because I've been on the receiving end
I know the pain she will go through
Tis harder for me to take a heart and rend
Than to have my heart broken in two
And certainly she will eventually mend
But for now we'll be colored blue.

The End

The time will come when the time will be
That my days on this earth will be over
I haven't decided if it's ashes for me
Or be buried to fertilize the clover.

I hope I have the chance for my final farewells
But unknown will be my condition
If I do then I'll shout them through the hills and the dells
Along with my final acts of contrition.

They say my life will flash before my eyes
It will be the ultimate rerun on TV
So I get to review my truths and my lies
Will I be watching it in high-def 3D?

Speaking of which my clothes and my hair
I have to watch how back then I was groomed?
I hope I am not judged on 70's styles, not fair!
Because if I am I am doomed!

I pray there is mercy in judging my fate
For I certainly haven't been rectitude
Yes I certainly hope I pass through that Gate
Which tho narrow I still might squeeze through.

I have no clue how God takes me home
No idea of where or when
So I guess now is the time to write this poem
Since there probably won't be time at the end.

Tillie

As Tillie steps out she's looking swell
    Every day she's the same exact story
All the boys love her, that you can tell
    Their praises to Tillie are adulatory
Even the boys who have no chance in hell
    Hey - no guts no glory!

In a halter top or a t-shirt in tie-dye
    Doesn't matter what Tillie wears
The girls all stand as she waltzes by
    Giving Tillie their evil glares
And the boys all form one long line and sigh
    On Tillie rests all of their stares.

If she has any strongly held views they're a mystery
    Tillie seems to sit on the fence
She can talk at length about cosmetology
    Tillie has a fabulous fashion sense
But in matters of geometry or trigonometry
    Let's face it, Tillie is dense.

If she ever hungers or wants for a drink
    Tillie never has to pay
All she has to do is look at a boy and wink
    And Tillie's hand on his cheek she will lay
With her eyes she can connect with that special link
    Yes with the boys Tillie sure has a way.

And every place she goes, yes no matter where
    All the boys follow Tillie on cue
For they know in love and war all is fair
    And every week Tillie's boy is new
And the girls clutch their beaus to keep them there
    For Tillie's stolen quite more than a few.

Now don't you fret about her at all
    Tillie will suffer little if any strife
She knows just what she wants in Life's Grand Ball
    Tillie knows just what she wants in her life
She'll meet a millionaire who's handsome and tall
    And he'll make Tillie his trophy wife.

Image in the Mirror

The face looking back in the reflective glass
Shows the lines and creases of age
And the body is so far from its youthful class
By any measuring gauge.

I remember events that happened to me
Throughout all of my yesteryear
For in my mind I can plainly see
And every event is oh so clear.

My mind tells me that I am the same
As I was all those years ago
My body with all of its aches and pain
Says maybe that isn't quite so.

I have learned that there is no fountain of youth
Not even a small little geyser
Events seemed to happen yesterday, but in truth
I'm much older and hopefully wiser.

Looking back through my lifelong lineage
My memories to the facts remain true
And so I know who **I** am image,
But image...who are you?

No More, No More

Against love I promised and I swore
Love no more, no more
    (Love so blue, so blue.)

Found love and promised just once more
That's what I swore, I swore.
    (Love so new, so new.)

Seemed love would last and be here to stay
Happiness is on the way, the way.
    (Love so true, so true.)

In between love and me something got in the way
Love just will not stay, not stay.
    (Love no clue, no clue.)

Three Love Shorts (1)

The Perfect Woman

A little more, a little less, add some of this, don't add that
    Been experimentin' and doing some cookin'
But I always seem to strike out at bat
    With the recipe for the perfect woman.

The Things I Do

I'm in and out of love so fast
    The Love Carousal goes round and round
Stepping on so soon after the last
    When I stumbled to the ground.

Why for love do I do the things that I do
    Why can't my love life show more civility?
I guess about me I've learned something new
    In that I'm not immune to stupidity.

A Tall Tale

They say that "It is better to have loved and lost
   Than to have never loved at all."
I ask who it is that measured this cost
   And started this tale so tall.

He probably never has felt that knife
   That love can sometimes be
He probably creates greeting cards in his working life
   And can't elsewhere sell his poetry

Different Times

I saw you walking casually down the street
    While I casually walked the other side
I recognized you and my heart skipped a beat!
    While in me past stirrings stirred inside.
It has been more than thirty years I knew
    Since we graduated on that high school stage
I fondly and many times think of you
    Do you think of me? No, you've probably turned the page.

I remember all those kisses we sweetly shared
    At night, while stars circled us above
And all those times our souls we bared
    I don't know, was it deep romance or was it puppy love?
We could not guess that it would be over so soon
    All that we vowed and promised in that age
It all ended on that June afternoon
    It all ended on that stage.

So I watched you walk in perfect stride
    And me standing there I know you didn't see
Should I say hello? Would you make small talk or push me aside?
    Or possibly much worse...would you not even remember me?
Holding memories dear I let you pass
    And friends tell me that no one is to blame
That for over thirty years I've dated many a fair lass
    And shocked when told, that you also find lasses fair game.

Downward Spiral

Sadly when I hear the news today
It's mostly violence and hatred I see
It seems as though we have lost our way
And a shroud of doom begins circling me.

Wishing these images out of my mind - oh that I could!
Of the violent rioting, looting, arsonist fires
And they taught that man was basically good?
Boy...those ancient Greeks were such liars!

The more I look round me the more that I find
Deep into the pit we are sinking
Wait, they really came here to save mankind?
What were that Virgin and Infant thinking?

It seems that we all have taken our side
Lessening the chasm is now our great riddle
It's sad that the canyon is so deep and so wide
Since the truth usually lies in the middle.

We seem to be ruled by a new Golden Rule
That violence can be a tool used for gain
If we seek common ground we're labeled a fool
And being canceled or harmed is our bane.

This all seemed to happen exceptionally fast
As if our society went on a great bender
It seems we regressed to a very violent past
And this certainly holds true for both gender.

So in trying to ignore our fads and the cads
In gazing over our country's great masses
I ask, where went all of the kind and good lads?
What happened to all the fair lasses?

Feelings For The Goddess

Aye Goddess when I think of us it always seems
   The image of you fiercely sets my heart burning
You warm me more than the sunlight beams
   The emotions inside me you send rapidly churning
So let me tell you how you fit in my dreams
   And also of my longing and yearning

As a vagabond dreams of his next place to roam
   And as an infant dreams of a warm blanket so new
As a soldier dreams of leaving the front for home
   And as an actor dreams of saying his lines all on cue
As a poet dreams of writing the next great poem
   Yea Goddess, that's how I dream of you.

As the office worker longs for that weekend of fun
   And as a gourmet longs for that meal so fine
As a beachcomber longs for a day filled with sun
   And as a connoisseur longs for that spectacular wine
As a marathon runner longs for a very fast run
   Yea Goddess, that's how I long for you to be mine.

As a mountaineer yearns for that mountain so high
   And as a tea sommelier yearns to collect the finest tea
As a pilot yearns for that clear blue sky
   And as a landlocked sailor yearns for the sea
As a baker yearns to bake the prize winning pie
   Yea Goddess, that's how I yearn for thee.

Closure

Her first kiss to him was so sublime
She previously declined at least once or more
And so he wondered why she chose this time
And not those times before?

Was there something special about this day
That would make her seek him out?
He never expected to meet this way
Tho he knew what this was about.

He knew his cares would soon be unburdened
As he met her face to face
And he saw that she was bound and determined
Dressed in her black and tatted lace.

He knew soon his racing heart would rest
And deep peace would finally come
His perspiring would end after reaching its crest
When that first sweet kiss was done.

Tenderly placing her kiss she sighed
When she finished he exhaled his last breath
For "she" was Death personified
And her's was the sweet Kiss of Death

Surprise!

I took a drive with you today
The weather being nice and warm
And as we drove along our way
We saw the sun, no sign of any storm.

I was actually surprised you got in the car
As I pulled up by your side
But I long admired you from afar
And so I offered you that ride.

We really talked and got to know
Each other as we drove along
And through our hair the wind did blow
As the radio played our favorite song.

So there was the trouble prone guy and society
girl - the two of us
Boy we must have been a sight!
We walk on different paths in life and thus
Was I wrong to think a spark just might ignite?

But I guess I mentioned something bad
Because you got out and stopped our roamin'
Yeah, you made quite a fuss and got really mad
When you found out the car was stolen.

So What Went Wrong? (1)

It Doesn't Add Up

We learned that math is very strict
    Summing two plus two gets four
The result will always equal that
    And neither less nor more

My life has never worked like that
    It is very different for me
When I add up the two and two
    My answer's always three.

And so I go through life like that
    Always adding wrong the math
Which makes me face the wild unknown
    Being forced off the beaten path.

Sleep Easy

The marble roofs lie above the ground
    Their inhabitants lie six feet under
We cry and pine and moan their fate
    But at times I look and wonder.

I think that they are the lucky ones
    Better off than us above
Their fate is known and there they lie
    No more having to deal with love.

Sea Life Hierarchy

They said the world is my oyster
So they told me when I was young
Work hard and all the accolades
From my neck they would be strung.

Life never really came out that way
And looking over what I am
Instead of the world being an oyster
It seems much more like a clam.

The Dream

I fell in love with you last night
When you slipped in to my dreams
You must have rode that silvery light
That make up those silvery moon beams
Floating through the fabric left then right
You found access through the seams.

The dream itself made little sense
As most dreams seldom do
You came in dancing then you left, whence
I know not where off to
But you kissed and held me, hence
That's when I fell in love with you.

And it still was dark when I awoke
So I lay there in my bed
And like an artists's master stroke
The dream lay vivid in my head
And while it faded as dawn broke
My love for you was wed.

I know you didn't dream of me
For that's not the way dreams work
And I know I won't again you see
For this time was just a quirk
But my love for you will now always be
In my subconscious it will perk.

Dinner With The Goddess

The date is set so it's time to plan
You are taking the Goddess to dinner!
So what type of food is she a fan?
What venue makes the evening a winner?

"Well how about parmesan or cacciatore chicken?
Over the menu's pasta items we'll roam."
Oh come on! You know the woman is pure bred Italian
She gets all of that at home!

"Okay, maybe a hamburger and an order of fries
Or else some tacos to brighten her mood?"
I really don't think that's very wise
You're trying to win her by ordering fast food?

"Well let me think about some other cuisine...
There's Greek, German and French you know."
Ah yes, the olive oil and cheese and sausage scene
And as for French, I'd advise you to avoid escargot.

"So how do I keep her from getting bored?
To impress her what do I do?"
Just take her to a nice place that you can afford
Remember, she's going because she's interested in YOU.

So listen, don't worry about the menu or seating
Just treat her as a lady of great prize
And don't worry about what you yourself will be eating
You'll be too busy devouring her with your eyes.

Thirty Years

For thirty years their star shone bright
They were the highlight of the town
They dined and danced all through the night
At every social event uptown.

It seemed that they knew everyone
As they greeted everyone by name
They spread good cheer and then when done
To other venues they spread the same.

The jokes they told seemed always new
And the stories that they would tell!
Their friends just sat and admired the two
Being a little envious as well.

His love for her was legend to all
And she reciprocated in kind
In their early years their hearts felt the call
No greater love will you ever find.

But as the late nights ended he knew
That she would soon be leaving him
And soon he would be leaving too
As the morning light dawned dim.

For as dawn broke, came then his tears
Things aren't always as they seem
For events in the night during those thirty years
Only happened in his dream.

Eighteen

At eighteen years I knew everything
I was certainly a sage
No one could tell me anything
As I was eighteen years of age.

At twenty eight how wise was I
Went to college and married too
I never asked of what or why
At twenty eight would you?

At thirty eight my status grew tall
And my age never bothered me
Never looked for any "writing on the wall"
For I was only thirty eight you see.

At forty eight my fame grew more
Against many obstacles I won
I had no fear of what lay in store
And at forty eight was proud of all I'd done.

At fifty eight I knew the truth
In that I was at my apex then
And I knew way more than all the youth
But oh….. to be eighteen again.

This poem first published in The Healing Muse, *Volume 22, a publication of* The Center for Bioethics *and Humanities, Upstate University Hospital.*

Erotica

I met an old friend while at the store
And I saw him look at my hand.
So I said let me tell you of a story and more
About a lovely day on the sand.

I met her on the beach on a warm summer's day
And the connection between us turned gold
To a secret cove we stole our way
As events quickly began to unfold.

The feelings between us started to rise
We both knew this was a win-win
And as we stared deep into each other's eyes
That's when the physical connection kicked in.

The kissing and fondling became very hot
And we quickly removed all our clothing
A normal day at the beach? Certainly not!
With our passions explosively emoting.

So I took my finger and traced her skin
From her cheek to her bare breast to her knee
She smiled and moaned from deep within
And when I finished she started on me.

Then came the whimpering and also the crying
The squealing was next to break free
And I mustn't forget the gasping and sighing
Yes, all of that came forth from me!

From there it was a blur, I don't remember much
I know my vision went into a spin
Oh, and also the panting and climaxes and such
With plenty of "OH YES!"'s thrown in.

After we finished, we picked up our clothes
Looked over at each other and then,
Locking our bodies from nose to toes
We started all over again.

So there we were as the sun started to set
Lying there while the tide rolled in
It washed away all of our well earned sweat
It cleansed us of our sin.

When we finally finished we slowly rose
And I walked her back to her car
Were we sated? Yes, pretty much I suppose
But with no idea of how long or how far.

So I see you are looking at what I have in my hand
Yes for her my feelings still linger
These flowers thank her for that day on the sand
And I'm proud to wear this ring on my finger.

Lady of Sorrow

Lady, Lady, you walk the night
Thy soul bereft of any light
Please tell us why you act thus so
Please share with us thy tale of woe
Can it be love-borne pain within
Or willful, vile, mortal sin?

Lady, Lady, alone you walk
You never smile, you never talk
Thou never missed a night to go
Be it stars or rain or driven snow
You walk until the dawn's first light
When hence you disappear from sight.

Lady, Lady, torn by strife
Hast thou given up on life?
You walk about with tear stained eyes
Were these caused by truths or lies?
Causing thee your nightly gait
With endless pain that won't abate.

Lady, Lady, Queen of Sorrow
You walk today, you'll walk tomorrow
Cursed to trod the roads of pain
Thy grieving tears will never wane
What does the future hold for thee?
What other future can there be.

Lady, Lady, through the years
You paid your penance with your tears
Thy grieving heart beats in thy chest
Thy hands are clasped upon thy breast
Repent your anguished soul within
God will forgive you of your sin.

Mors Voluntaria

Here, lying in unconsecrated ground we condemn
Those stigmatized because of their stealth
No one went and took their lives from them
All of them went and took it themself.

We call them cowards and say they are selfish
Tho we never felt the pain of their shoes
To severely suffer or be granted a death wish
Cursed, with no other option to choose.

We chide them and scold them and tell them with force
"You're ruining God's plan for you!"
So do we let an infection take its natural course?
Not us, we take an antibiotic or two.

So here is Walter who before he ended his life
He lay there all day paralyzed
Somehow one day he managed to grab a knife
Slashing his wrists he bled out and died.

On that gravestone yonder you see Susan's name
You won't convince me her death was her fault
For they whisper and say her mind was never the same
After she suffered that sexual assault.

And there lies Mike whose only real sin
Was that he was born a hundred years late
They died back then before excruciating pain set in
Now modern medicine won't give them that fate.

So I'll not stand here and judge or lecture these few
Telling them Heaven thinks their souls are a loss
Because I'm pretty sure it was also for them too
That Jesus went and died on that cross.

Somewhere

They say out there is a lass for me
Someone special that I will meet
Of her all I have to do is see
And she will sweep me off my feet
A bonnie lass who will certainly be
The one to make my life complete.

This lass I'm told was made for me
And that I was made for her
With looks and locks lying pleasurably
And a personality demure
A match so perfect it cannot but be
Made in heaven as it were.

They say this lass will make my day
And as I take her by her hand
That we'll walk the paths of life's byway
As the hourglass drips its sand
And this will all come true they say
Just be patient, you can't rush a wedding band.

So I'm glad there is a lass so fair
Who for me she'll shed a tear
And above all the other lads she'll care
And hold my substance dear
It's just a shame that she is off somewhere
And a shame that I am here.

Astronomically Speaking

When we were teens we'd lie on the grass
We cuddled up to one another
There we were, the lad and the lass
Observing the night sky with each other.

We saw the North Star and planets in the sky
The constellations and nebulas too
And talked Greek mythology as the stars went by
That's how the stars were named we knew.

Invariably we talked about places on Earth
Of the things we would do and see
Our adventures would be filled with merriment and mirth
Together, you and me.

But Life called us to go our separate way
And I have no clue as to where you are
We have lived our own lives as we slowly turn gray
But up there we still have our North Star.

Did you ever do any of the plans that we had?
I did and saw the people, the cultures, the weather!
And while I enjoyed the time it is still a bit sad
We did not visit those places together.

So when you turn your eyes to the heavens and see
Yes, I see the same heavens as you
I hope you take some time and think of me
As I look upwards and think of you.

Springtime

When Springtime blossoms in the air
And sweet lasses outside sway
Tis time to pick a lady fair
To give my heart away.

This highly sweet and tender soul
Picked carefully by me
Will be highly suited for the role
As no other lass can be.

This lady plays a special part
As when my new love crashes
She's next in line to stomp my heart
And give it forty lashes.

People think for me it's sad
When ladies are resistant
But I don't think it's all that bad
At least this lad's consistent.

So now when Cupid in the Spring
Sends arrows as he may
I just really wish for him to bring
One arrow out my way.

Shades of Gray

I knew of virtue as a tot
  Both good and bad were a simple lot
Wrong was wrong and right was right
  Black was black and white was white
Hot was different than the cold
  As silver's shine is not like gold.
Day was day and night was night
  The black hat different from the white.

I'm older now and so have seen
  The two extremes and in between
The hot and cold are blended warm
  It's cloudy now not sun nor storm
While dark and day become twilight
  Dawn is a mix of the morn and night
Each smoky, shadowy, grayish hue
  Did not exist and now they do.

In seeing between the two extremes
  It is hard to judge mankind it seems
For while we all may talk the talk
  We fail at times to walk the walk
So who are the Saints, who are the Sinners,
  Who are the Losers, who are the Winners
Who will proceed through that narrow Gate?
  Those shades of gray will decide our fate.

Sounds Like A Plan

Life is very hard it seems
  Filled up with hopes and wishes
But broken promises and the dreams
  Are strewn like broken dishes.

We never know how life will be
  Or how it will turn out
Will it all be laughter that we see
  Or will sadness come about?

Do we live on time we borrow?
  Will we seek the day so bright?
Will we laugh today and cry tomorrow
  Seeking solace in the night?

Will we feel a bit unequal,
  With our moral compass lacking,
And will our days feel like a sequel
  Our ship, is it east or westward tacking?

Will days for us be a song and dance
  Or will we cry upon our pillow?
Will we take a solid oak tree stance
  Or be the human weeping willow?

So when Life's tricks play on our fear
  And throw us off our track
When it seems Life bit us on our rear
  Just turn around and bite him back.

Three Love Shorts (2)

Pretty Simple

What happens to us unlucky in love
Those alone all through the night?
Does the sun still shine from up above
Though our roses show some blight?

What happens again and again as we try
When we step to the plate as the batter?
Well we are born we live and then we die
And I guess that ends the matter.

That Special Day

Valentine's Day is here again
It has come once more our way
But for those of us who are unattached
It is just another day.

The special day at least for me
And it really does not fail
Is the day that comes after Valentine's Day
When all of that candy goes on sale.

Yeah, That Too

My friends just shake their heads at me
And tell me no one is to blame
That there are thousands of others in my boat
And they all do feel the same.

They repeat their time worn words of wisdom
That should make me feel swell
But Ha! I proved them wrong again
Because I'm unlucky at cards as well!

I Grew Up

I came across some nursery rhymes
I knew them all by heart
But they didn't read like olden times
In fact they gave me quite a start.

Jack jumped over the candlestick
But was that candle tall and lit?
And hey diddle diddle the cat sure played that fiddle
But the dish and spoon didn't like it.

The old man snoring with the head injury
He appears to be in a coma
And the baby rocking at the top of that tree
Predicting a fall would not take a diploma.

The little old lady living in that shoe
Whipping her poor hungry kids seems mean
And Little Bo Peep and Little Boy Blue
Were the worst shepherds I've ever seen.

Now a little spider came crawling around
Causing such consternation to Miss Muffet?
I guess Itsy Bitsy Spider would have really just drowned
And that would have been the end of it.

These rhymes get more impossible
As I read them page by page
Do you think it just might be possible
That I get more cynical with age?

So What Went Wrong? (2)

Doomed

Doctors treat and cure our ills
The clergy save our souls
Lawyers go and make our wills
The road crews fill pot holes.

Pilots guide a plane in flight
Dancers swing and sway
And as for me I sit and write
And rhyme my life away.

Gone But Not Forgotten

We hardly use a landline phone
Phonebooks are tossed aside
Phonographs sit in closets now
With typewriters by their side.

Mules no longer ply the towpath
Steam engines can't compete
So I hope to finish out my days
Before they find me obsolete.

I Found It!

I never was an athlete
I never knew real fame
I never was a muscleman
The Dean's List never knew my name.

I never made the tons of money
In my chosen profession
But finding that elusive rhyming word?
Ah, now you know my obsession!

The Cause

See over there the highly vibrant and independent nation
A land filled with peaceful, kind and ordinary peoples
Their houses, shops, factories and the usual churches' steeples
Suddenly attacked and put upon by a massive desecration.

See in their midst the stalwart President not swaying like a reed
Though he knows he is centered in the mongrel dog's crosshair
He will not run nor hide from the attacking Russian Bear
He is a hero, made not born, a very special breed.

See the people trade in the usual tools they use
To defend they turn them in for guns and other such munitions
Artists, writers, engineers, accountants, plumbers and electricians
All fighting hard together as one for the Freedom that
they choose.

See the loving couple marry and pledge their love to the heavens
Where now will they go and spend their lovely honeymoon?
They willingly go and join the front lines all too very soon
As both still pledge their undying love but now carry AK-47's.

See their athletes stand and play a very different game
They make their stand though in this game they know they are behind
The arena they are competing in is a totally different state of mind
A loss before and a loss right now is nowhere near the same.

See the sons from other lands come to help Ukraine fight the foe
Inspired by Ukraine's bravery they come from near and far
These sons cannot just watch events unfold at some local corner bar
Stand tall ye sons of nations as you help the winds of Freedom blow!

Even as the world's tears fall upon the Earth like rain
See Freedom's torch held very high as its shining light burns bright
This is the goal and dream for which all good people fight
Raise your fists and shout "We stand as one! Freedom for Ukraine!"

Ten-Hut!

You remember the day you brought him home
All wrapped up in a blanket so warm
So tiny, so frail, you were his protective dome
Giving him shelter from any storm.

You remember all of the "firsts" in his early years
The walking and talking then school
All of the laughter and all of the tears
As you taught him the Golden Rule.

You remember every milestone in his life it seems
Even though time through the years quickly ran
You knew all of his friends, his hopes and his dreams
Before you knew it he was a grown up young man.

You remember the day he said he was going to sign up
He would stand on that wall he avowed
You never knew why he chose to drink from that cup
But of his decision, yes, you were proud.

You remember when it was time for him to go
Your worries you tried to hide
You hoped your concern on your face did not show
But after he left, you prayed and you cried.

Now you watch the folded flag carried your way
On a day you will remember like no other
The nation owes you a debt which it can never
repay
For now you are a Gold Star Mother.

*This poem first read in public at the New York State Gold
Star Mothers Convention in Auburn, New York on
April 26th, 2024.*

Two Versions

A. His Version

I took a walk in the open air
   Taking rest on a park bench seat
It was the first time ever that I saw her there
   The space between us about thirty feet
And I studied her up and down with care
   In the all too hot and humid heat.

I could tell about the same age we were
   Our middle years we already passed through
And age was very kind to her
   With both her looks and body too
And while she wore a faint smile I was sure
   That she held a faint streak of blue.

I saw no ring upon her hand
   So I knew that now she was not wed
Did past divorce remove that band
   Or was it a straight single life she led?
And was there a man to make life grand
   Or was she maybe still searching instead?

She looked liked a woman I could get to know
   Her waist my arm could go around
She seemed like she would go with the flow
   With no hint of a temperament unsound
Would our friends get along? Hopefully so
   And would she pet my cat when she came 'round?

And as these thoughts floated about
   I searched for words to say
I opened my mouth but nothing came out
   So she really had no reason to stay
And of me again I failed to tout
   Whence she got up and walked away.

B. Her Version

I took a walk in the open air
   Standing near a park bench seat
It was the first time ever that I saw him there
   The distance less than twenty feet
And I studied him up and down with care
   In the sunny but pleasant heat.

I'm guessing close to the same age we were
   Though his middle years he already passed through
And age seemed good to the sprightly sir
   He was thin and seemed energetic too
And while he wore a faint smile I was sure
   In him there was a faint streak of blue.

I saw no ring upon his hand
  So I knew now he was not wed
Did past divorce remove that band
  Or was it always a single life he led?
And was there a lady to make life grand
  Or was he maybe still searching instead?

He looked liked a man I could get to know
  My waist I would like his arm around
A steady man who would go with the flow
  With no hint of a temperament unsound
Would our friends get along? Hopefully so
  And would he pet my dog when he came 'round?

And I wished as my thoughts floated about
  That I was a woman who always knew what to say
He seemed to open his mouth but nothing came out
  So I guess I had no reason to stay
And of me again I failed to tout
  So sadly I walked away.

With Apologies To My Fellow Man

Please judge me not for I did sin
On the paths I walked through life
I have seen at times you just can't win
When marching to that drum and fife.

Life can be hard and toss a curve
Even change a core belief
And in my attempt to duck and swerve
I dealt my fellow man some grief.

I did not mean to cause such pain
To my fellow man you see
But in trying hard to avoid life's rain
I only thought of me.

Moments like this seem so rife
Where our temper gets away
Where we cast our anger at said life
And our fellow man gets in the way.

I only know when me I view
I have seen both beauty and beast
I have seen the best that I can do
And I have also seen the least.

So while some enjoy their lifelong trip
And only see good float by
I know there is truth in what others quip
Life's a bitch and then you die.

The Jury's Still Out

Two lads did vie, their hearts were sold
  To a lass with airs about
One lad had pockets flush with gold
  I was the lad without
So down between us the gauntlet tossed
  To win her hand and wed
But for the hand we vied I lost
  And he took her to his bed
I had not heard of them in years
  Until shocked by news I read
It seems the lass took gun in tears
  And left the lad for dead.

The DA painted a picture bad
  Said she knew he wanted divorce
So instead of losing every cent she had
  She saved her wealth of course
Her lawyer claimed it self defense
  "You must free her!" was his plea
He said tho sad it all made sense
  For she was a battered wife you see.

From knowing them and all I read
   I do not care who the guilty be
But for all the words her lawyer said
   The jury did not agree
I know not what I can take and save
   From this woeful tale of strife
A heart broke lad, a lad in grave
   The lass doing thirty five to life
And in my state of mind so stressed
   I sit thinking reflectively
Would all our lives be better blessed
   If she had only chosen me.

When Worlds Collide

I watched you walk in gracefully
You so quickly caught my eye
You talked with your hands so easily
I let out a longing sigh.

Your face, your hair, those ruby lips
Light the room just like the sun
And if Helen launched a thousand ships
I'm sure you'd launch a thousand and one.

I long to tell my feelings and such
But the signs I know are few
A smile, a nod, an accidental touch
For now, is all I can hope from you.

But I really need not write a rhyme
As anybody can plainly see
For when you stand and stroll each time
You write your own poetry.

My friends tell me it is useless to yearn
When I cannot tell you this without sound
I cry out to them "I'll learn, I'll learn!"
To your essence my heart is bound.

So of my feelings you have no clue
But my dreams around you have swirled
And one day I will sign my love to you
When I can partake of your silent world.

A Wasted Moon

Yonder over are the Hills of Hope
  Towards which I keep on going
Traversing up and down each slope
  Over ragged streams there flowing
And there on hands and knees to grope
  While the wind never ceases blowing.

The search for love is never kind
  A path strewn with brambly thorns
The spirit it crushes and then will grind
  Lost innocence it never mourns
And on towards pain in heart and mind
  It laughs and throws its scorn.

When the daylight gets on towards dark
  And the heaven's stars rise high
When lovers turn out to embark
  And the night owl sends its cry
The lonely take in deep breath stark
  And let out a mournful sigh.

I alone is a lonely sight
  Sadly there is no we
And the lonely heart beats through the night
  As I look up and I see
A romantic moon giving off its light
  But sadly not for me.

Win Some, Lose Some

So why does it seem everywhere I go
That I run right into this pair?
The girl that set my heart all aglow
And her new boyfriend walking there?

It's bad enough I lost the fight
But Cupid must think it's fun
To keep sending those two into my sight
To emphasize the fact we are done.

All the dances I escorted her to
She now gyrates 'round him
And the open kissing in public view
Done in spite or done on whim?

At the beach and at the bar
All the places we did go
Turn my head and there they are
Putting on their little show.

I can only shake my head and try
To move onward from this mess
But that takes time which is why
I am still morose I guess.

So it's hard not to dwell on him who won
And I know she is free to choose
But when all the words are said and done
Damn it sucks to lose.

Setting It All Up

You met him in college and you weren't really sure
But he was persistent in asking you out
Slowly but surely from your shell he did lure
And your feelings for him turned about.

You did not rush as you slowly felt your way
Though he held a special place in your heart
And he grew on you with every passing day
Then you promised till death do you part

You lived in an apartment so cramped and so small
Filling it with furniture new
And while no space remained on floor or the wall
It was perfect for the two of you.

But you kept your eye on that mortgage rate
And looked for that home you sought
Now you could go out and celebrate
For your dream home you finally bought.

Buying some wine towards home you did run
A romantic dinner you made for your spouse
And over the week you both had some fun
As you christened each room in the house.

Now nine months later down there you're feeling soaked
And definitely not feeling alright
I'm afraid that yes, your water broke
Your life together starts changing tonight!

Memories From
A Simpler Time

Past the docks the river flows
As the last light starts to die
And upon the wind that gently blows
Sounds of music float on by.

As darkness falls across the land
And stars rise high in sight
The colored lights shine on the band
Pushing music into the night.

The patrons rise and start to move
Their bodies pulsing with the beat
And those not dancing sit and groove
As they sit there in their seat.

I listen to the music too
The tunes both slow and fast
I remember when the songs were new
Great memories from the past.

And as I listen the more I find
Things I'd forgotten long ago
Come drifting back into my mind
Giving me smiles as they go.

Somewhere pain inhabits the land
Somewhere else out there is sorrow
But tonight I listen to the band
And dream of past and not tomorrow.

The Veteran

I see the veteran standing there
As the flag is raised on high
With a silent, fixed, unbroken stare
He exhales a heavy sigh
And of his thoughts I wonder where
His faded memories lie.

Is he thinking of a bygone day
When a young man once he was?
And he chose the military as his way
Maybe for adventure 'twas?
Or maybe he felt it his duty say
Or maybe it was just because.

Maybe he thinks of battles fought
Whether on air or land or sea
And how very lucky he was he thought
In that hellish geography
To use the lessons he was taught
To stay alive most thankfully.

Or maybe he thinks of friends he knew
As they served far off somewhere
Both the men and women too
Whose luck ran out over there
Time turns their memory a faded hue
But of their memory he still does care.

He probably thinks of all of these
As he looks at that flagpole tall
And at the flag waving in the breeze
Knowing its history and all
To him I tip my hat with ease
For us he stood upon that wall.

The Duel

The sun is at its zenith high
And shines down on the street
I stand up with a weary sigh
Time for him and I to meet.

I swore an oath to protect this town
I wear this badge with pride
My white hat worn just like a crown
My gun holstered at my side.

This street of dirt is a peaceful sight
But nobody is it fooling
It has seen too many deadly fights
Very soon blood will be pooling

Beads of sweat form on my brow
To kill a man I'm torn
Will my life be ended now
Or will I wake up in the morn?

The streets are clear no one makes fuss
No townsfolk do I see
It's now between the two of us
Will it be him or me?

I give him one more chance to leave
But his hand goes to his gun
Of me are townsfolk soon to grieve
Or rejoice the fact I've won?

I do not feel the bullet's wrath
But I'm dead now just the same
At least ten times I've walked this path...
Boy, I stink at this video game.

Colors Of Fall

I stand and gaze upon the sight
  Of what used to be pure green
And it seemed so quick that overnight
  It became a colorful scene.

The green is gone and in its place
  Are the yellow, the orange, the red!
And this is how Fall shows its face
  Colorful tapestries we are fed.

Once the leaves begin their flight
  And softly float around
The colors once so high in sight
  Are transferred to the ground.

I see the children laugh and play
  Their games are Games of Fall
Each generation has been this way
  With the cold and leaves and all.

If I could stay and watch I would
  In warm jacket and long sleeves
But I've stood and stalled long as I could
  Time to go and rake those leaves.

To Two Greats

As I sit and ponder my long ago youth
    Stretching into a late teenage year
A transistor radio was my musical booth
    My 45's and cassettes I held dear.

While I certainly enjoyed many a band
    I was drawn towards individuals two
One would sing about mountainous land
    The other of true love and love blue.

We followed him on his rocky mountain high
    On his country roads he took us home
And goodbye again would make us sigh
    Fly away made our spirits roam.

She sang of love that had just begun
    And love unsure for all we knew
About hurting each other she sadly sung
    Goodbye to love some knew to be true.

Fame and fortune were eventually found
    But sadly their lives were cut short
Leaving their fans without any new sound
    Drifting like ships with no port.

So as I quietly sit and think upon
    How you both made my life less barren
I thank thee much Denver John
    God bless thee Carpenter Karen

A Weighty Balance

In my head my memories sift
  The minutes I start to squander
My conscious mind begins to drift
  My thoughts begin to wander.

My darkest times I think about
  Things I wish I did not see
Words and actions coming out
  I wish not came from me.

At the point I'm filled with dread
  Overwhelmed by sense of doom
A light shines brightly up ahead
  Which penetrates the gloom.

It illuminates my kindly deeds
  The cheer I've spread around
My works are planted like good seeds
  They sprout out from the ground.

I think of all my damning strife
  That defines the mean and gritty
I ponder all things in my life
  But life's not always pretty.

So once again I balance stark
  The good and bad I've done
But there is much more light than dark
  So I guess that I have won.

Ode To A Mother

Mother, Mother, I see you dance
Are your spirits soaring high perchance?
What causes you to kick up your heels
Your love of life and the way it feels?
The laughter in you overflows
Your joy your mirth it clearly shows.

Mother, Mother, I see you cry
I see the tear fall from your eye
Your children's pain you feel inside
Your arms you spread and open wide
To shield them from the hurt and such
You are only able to do so much.

Mother, Mother, I see you tired
All stressed out your nerves are wired
Running here and running there
Tomorrow running off somewhere
On the go from morn til night
To begin again with next day's light.

Mother, Mother I see you sleep
Some nights you smile some nights you weep
Sometimes good sleep will come your way
It gives you rest for another day
At other times you toss and turn
As thoughts within you twist and churn.

Mother, Mother I see you kneel
Before your God you pray with zeal
You ask for blessings upon your clan
Your son your daughter and your man
And for yourself you pray now too
Relax Dear Mother, God heareth you.

Time Is Distance

I met the woman of my dreams
And I would court her with desire
But I'm thirty years her elder seems
Which makes my longing dire.

We grew up thirty years apart
So we have little common ground
Without shared past how can we start?
Can the relationship be sound?

And in those thirty years it's true
I have seen more due to age
She hasn't seen what I have seen
For she's nowhere near that page.

While our likes and interests match
I have my big time fears
That although they match they cannot patch
And overcome those thirty years.

A lot of men don't think it's bad
Dating women far younger than they
But I'm old enough to be her dad
That might get in the way.

The eyes, brown hair, those puffy cheeks
So beautiful to me
But the mirror that I gaze into freaks
Gray hair is all I see.

I sit and think what could have been
If I was born around her time
Or she was born around me then
Would I have wrote a different rhyme?

So while it's sad I'm very sure
In vain for her I fell
But I only wish the best for her
I only wish her well.

And as I watch her when she nears
I think of this a lot
If I was thirty younger years
But sadly I am not.

The Never Ending Cycle

Seasons come and seasons go
As they repeat end on end
I know that this is thus, and so
They've become an old time friend.

I watch the farmer at his game
In his field across the road
And overall the work's the same
But each season has its mode.

In Spring the farmer drives his plow
His planters plant the seeds
And after this he takes his bow
Now rain is all he needs.

They say "Knee high by Fourth of July"
But I'm always surprised to see
That as the Summer flows on by
The corn towers over me.

In the Fall the stalks will brown
As harvest time is here
And all around this farmland town
The threshers gather near.

The Winter snow lies on the ground
Cut cornstalks peek on through
And grayish skies are all around
While cold winds blow on cue.

I've watched these fields over thirty years
As the seasons flow on past
Like a well oiled clock with precision gears
I will watch them till my last.

The Magician

Two worlds exist and live their days
   Distinct from one another
And they communicate in different ways
   So it's hard to converse with each other.

But to communicate they surely must
   Many times their worlds collide
And that is where interpreters are thrust
   On in to the fray they ride.

Whether using hands in manual sign
   Or of the spoken word
They interpret the sentence line by line
   With clear meaning and not inferred.

In business in medicine in the legal realm
   And also so much more
They ease the fear that can overwhelm
   When misunderstanding knocks at the door.

So now these worlds can interact
   Thanks to a very special breed
They came they saw and the simple fact
   They rise up and fill a need.

So by your word and by your hand
   These worlds you bind and tether
Stand proud ye interpreters across the land
   For you bring different worlds together.

The Argument

The friendship ends, the bonds undone
  And I honestly don't know why
What words were said, what actions done
  That made things go awry?

We hadn't known each other long
  Had good times before the strife
But now that things went horribly wrong
  You've blocked me from your life.

We sit at table and our hardness firms
  And consciously ignore one another
Two former friends on the best of terms
  Pretending we don't know each other.

If we could see a different view
  Looking from the other's side
Would again those bonds we had renew
  And override our stubborn pride?

Between us lies the age old song
　　Which prolongs our little fight
We both think that the other's wrong
　　We both think we are right.

We need to start those words to flow
　　But I can't take my own advice
To be the first is hard I know
　　It's so hard to break that ice.

So in all of life's insanity
　　I sit and mourn the friendship lost
In terms of human vanity
　　Pride has its ugly cost.

Here's To Friends

Another romance ends and thus
   Another shipwreck on my sea
There is no longer "we" or "us"
   There is only you and me
And how do I forget this fuss
   For something never meant to be?

I go for solace to my friends
   To commiserate my loss
They help me tie up all lose ends
   They help me bear my cross
That desert where my spirit mends
   They help me get across.

My friends will help me through any pain
   For they have been there too
They've been on board and rode that train
   For us it's nothing new
That's when I helped to keep them sane
   I kindly helped them through.

Not just love but in other crimes
    My friends came to my aid
And I to theirs in their desperate times
    Our friendship we displayed
With actions equal to nickels and dimes
    Our friendship dues we paid.

And that is what our friends are for
    To stand up by our side
To help us through bad times and more
    To wade through life's high tide
The good, the bad, what lays in store
    Together we will ride.

Masked

Upon the bridge with self disdain
  Would he do it? He did not know
A simple step would end his pain
  It would send him far below.
He thought about his wasted life
  One without redeeming value
The hurt cut through him like a knife
  His self worth he would devalue.

With an emptiness through life he trod
  His spirit only filled with sorrow
Many times he had prayed to his God
  To not let him wake tomorrow.
No one knew his pain within
  The crushing loneliness deep inside
Darkness slowly creeping in
  All those nights he lay and cried.

He pondered deeply as to his fate
  As he knew church teaching well
Could he still walk through that heavenly gate
  Or would he face the gates of hell?
Reflecting on these thoughts awhile
  He would give it one more day
He forced upon his face a smile
  Turned around and walked away.

Film At 11:00

On the dock under a morning sun
A rented kayak floating by me
I set out for adventure and some fun
Adventure came but the fun was not to be.

With one misstep I left firm land
As the kayak immediately capsized
With water deep I could not stand
No matter how I tried.

Thrashing and flailing my arms around
With water flying everywhere
A grip on dock could not be found
No safety anywhere.

I thought the time was nearing when
My days would cease to be
But a woman grabbed my leg and then
From savage sea she pulled me free.

I hope no child cameth near
To see sailing skills so faulty
And hopefully they did not hear
As my language turned quite salty.

So there I stood all dripping wet
For every eye to see
I sure did make their day I bet
As they told their friends of me.

Water is good the scientists say
The benefits are true and tried
But all it did for me that day
Was hurt my tender pride.

O sadly shined the sun that day
As I walked in squishy shoes
A water trail behind me lay
I hope this doesn't make the news.

The Queen Reigneth

The night began as the band started its sound
  The patrons had already arrived through the door
But the excitement and fun would not come around
  Until Miss Tonia took to the floor.

With clothes and shoes just made to dance
  An aura of confidence she exquisitely bore
When eyes fell on her it wasn't by chance
  As Miss Tonia's expertise worked the floor.

All of the dancers who were up on their feet
  Moved off to the side as for
Everyone knew they just couldn't compete
  When Miss Tonia was out on that floor.

With every movement defined done precisely in time
  A dancing machine right down to her core
All body movements done in rhythmical rhyme
  Miss Tonia soon controlled all the floor.

Pulsing to the beat she would twist and bend
   Letting her spirit ecstatically soar
Moving like a whirlwind from end to end
   Miss Tonia completely owning that floor.

We pondered of this our visual treat
   As we all wished we could have seen more
Memories and images lingering sweet
   Of Miss Tonia ruling that floor.

Now people will say that the band was pure light
   The best band that ever played they swore
And they will be the best band that is rocking the night
   As long as Miss Tonia is rocking that floor.

A Tearful Situation

The tears will start and soon will fall
   I've walked this path before
I've seen the writing on the wall
   So I know what lays in store
To do this isn't an easy call
   It makes me cry and more.

I still don't know of where to start
   Or where I should begin
In this there is no easy part
   There is no way to win
On this I look with heavy heart
   Sad emotions do creep in.

I cannot stall for very long
   As this task must soon be done
To put it off is surely wrong
   And no good for anyone
The sadness of a mournful song
   Through my soul does run.

I wish that I could put a stop
   To this strife that soon will be
But soon that other shoe will drop
   Between this triangle of three
The onion on the counter top
   The paring knife and me.

Two Versions Revisited

A. *His Version*

She was already sitting at the park bench seat
   Where I have seen her many times before
And I had always hoped each other we'd greet
   Maybe talk and walk or more
But all of my plans had met with defeat
   For us nothing seemed to be in store.

Sadly I thought I'd leave and that's when
   I heard a voice come from deep inside me
It yelled "You fool! Don't let her go again!
   Don't blow this opportunity"
I blurted out "Nice pink socks" and thought then
   Socks? Really? What a dork she thinks I must be!

She opened her mouth but out came no sound
   And for sure I thought we were done
But then a mirthful laugh inside her she found
   And together we started laughing as one
I moved closer to her as the bench I came 'round
   We sat for an hour in the all too hot sun.

So after we talked in sunshine bright
   She suggested we walk about
The inside of me was still very tight
   If she'd date me I still had a doubt
But I asked her to go to dinner tonight
   And from her lips a yes came out.

When the sun came up and rose today
  I thought it will be the same old same
But I was wrong I'm happy to say
  To me romance finally came
Thanks to that park bench seat of gray
  My love finally has a first name.

B. Her Version

He was walking towards the park bench seat
  Where I have seen him many times before
I often thought of how we could greet
  Maybe talk and walk or more
But the plans I planned all met with defeat
  For us nothing seemed to be in store.

Sadly I thought I'd leave and that's when
  I heard a voice come from deep inside me
It yelled "Do something! Don't let him go again!
  Don't blow this opportunity"
He suddenly said "Nice pink socks" and I thought then
  He likes my favorite socks! A gentleman he must be!

I tried to respond but out came no sound
  And for sure I thought we were done
But then a mirthful laugh inside me I found
  And together we started laughing as one
I moved closer to him as the bench he came 'round
  We sat for an hour in the very pleasant sun.

So after we talked in sunshine bright
　　It was my idea that we walk about
He seemed a little nervous and very tight
　　Maybe about us he still had a doubt?
But he asked me to go to dinner tonight!
　　I was so excited the yes barely came out.

When the sun came up and rose today
　　I thought everything would be the same
But everything looks so different I'd say
　　Now that to me romance finally came
Thanks to that park bench seat of grey
　　My love finally has a first name.

That's All Folks

The early eve turns into late
   And the fire dies on down
Shadows formed by its glow abate
   With streetlights on in town.

It's time for us to take our leave
   And to go our separate way
The memories that tonight we weave
   I hope with us they'll stay.

I'm glad we had this time to share
   To do again are hopes I hold
And at that future when and where
   I'll have more verses to unfold.

Title Index

Index

Title Index

First Line of Poem Index

First Line of Poem Index

ABOUT THE AUTHOR:

Steve Ziemba spends most of his time masquerading as a Business Manager for a department at a university in Syracuse, New York. While primarily educated in the finance and computer fields (he has an MBA and two Bachelors Degrees in Business Public Management and Management Information Systems), he also pursues other interests such as learning ASL, motorcycle riding and various homesteading hobbies. He has spent time in the past volunteering at his town food pantry and his village library. Most of the ideas for his poetry comes from his observations of everyday life. He can be reached at smpz30@yahoo.com.

www.ingramcontent.com/pod-product-compliance
Lightning Source LLC
Chambersburg PA
CBHW052134090426
42741CB00009B/2082